A COMPLIMENTARY REVIEW COPY, FALL 1969

A DEFENDERS OF FREEDOM BOOK

Omar Nelson Bradley: The Soldiers' General

BY COL. "RED" REEDER
ILLUSTRATED BY HERMAN B. VESTAL

ABOUT THE BOOK: The illustrious career of a brilliant military leader is covered in detail in this biography of General Omar N. Bradley. From his youthful years at West Point, through his accomplishments during World War II, to his position as Chairman of the Joint Chiefs of Staff, Bradley's life has been filled with courage, hard work, modesty, and a sense of humor, all of which are portrayed clearly in this book. This is one of Garrard's DEFENDERS OF FREEDOM books, which features the life stories of fascinating characters, both contemporary and historical, and reconstruct with vivid detail and action many of the important crises in history.

Subject classification: Social Studies, American History, Biography

Sub-classification: World War II, Military History, Reading, Information

ABOUT THE AUTHOR: Col. "Red" Reeder has been associated with the Army all his life. He was an outstanding athlete at West Point and directed athletics for the Army in the Canal Zone. He began writing seriously after he was sent to Guadalcanal in 1942. His report of his trip, entitled "Fighting on Guadalcanal" was a classic of war reporting. More than one million copies of it were printed and were used as training manuals. His military service extended until his retirement in 1947. He led a regiment ashore in Normandy on D-Day and was seriously wounded on the sixth day of the invasion. For 20 years he served as Special Assistant to the Director of Athletics at West Point. He is the author of many books, including four for Garrard.

Reading Level: Grade 5

112 pages . . . 6⅞ x 9⅛

SBN 8116-4602-5

Interest Level: Grades 4–7

Publisher's Price: $2.69

Illustrated with photographs and 2-color art; full-color jacket; reinforced binding; index

GARRARD PUBLISHING COMPANY

I have known Colonel Russell "Red" Reeder since he was a Cadet at West Point in the early 1920's while I was an instructor there. I noted his athletic ability, his engaging personality, and his talent for leadership.

In the 1930's Red and I often played golf together and shot quail in Georgia. He was a fine sportsman and a wonderful companion.

Prior to the Normandy invasion, I visited the 12th Infantry Regiment, which Red commanded. I knew it would be well led on D-Day.

Red received a bad wound on the sixth day of the fighting. Even after he had been evacuated, I continued to read reports on his fine leadership on the beaches and in the tough hedgerow country. I am convinced, had he not been wounded, he would have been, at the very least, a Major General.

It is unfortunate for our country that we lost Red Reeder as a combat leader. But it is fortunate that he recovered and devoted years to helping the West Point Cadets. He has also dedicated himself to encouraging young people to read history that is part of our heritage.

Omar N Bradley

Omar N. Bradley
General of the Army

KARSH, OTTAWA

OMAR NELSON
BRADLEY
The Soldiers' General

BY COLONEL "RED" REEDER

ILLUSTRATED BY HERMAN B. VESTAL

GARRARD PUBLISHING COMPANY
CHAMPAIGN, ILLINOIS

FOR

Scott Reeder McCutchen

and his grandmother

Dort Darrah Reeder

Maps by Henri A. Fluchere

J
923.5
B

Contents

1. West Point

The pitcher wound up. A high fast ball zinged toward the batter's face. The batter, New Cadet Omar Bradley, moved his heavy jaw slightly out of the way. The ball grazed his chin and popped into the catcher's mitt.

The West Point baseball coach Sam Strang Nicklin howled at the pitcher, "Mister! Get the ball over the plate! I want to see this boy hit."

Young Omar Bradley, six feet and stringy, ground his spikes into the clay of the batter's box. He was completely relaxed while his deep-set eyes glared at the pitcher.

Again the ball sped straight at Omar. It twisted ever so slightly, then sank toward the dirt. Omar Bradley stepped straight ahead. His bat lashed forward and smacked the ball as it crossed the plate. The crack of the bat echoed against Cullum Hall in deep left field. The center fielder moved back fast but not quickly enough. Omar tore around the bases and came into the plate standing up.

"Very good!" Sammy Strang said.

A bugler near the West Academic Building sounded the jerky notes of "Recall." The 30 plebes at summer baseball practice gathered their equipment quickly and piled it near the home team bench. A first classman trotted out from the grandstand. "All right, you plebes!" he called. "Fall in!"

"Hey, mister," Sammy Strang said. "Can you spare me Mister Bradley for a few minutes?"

"Certainly," the first classman said.

Twenty-nine plebes in gray baseball suits left the diamond in a column of two's and double-timed toward cadet barracks.

Sammy Strang sank to the bench and motioned Omar to sit beside him. The coach's tight-fitting gray jersey was dark with perspiration. It was a sultry August afternoon.

Cadet Bradley, lean and tan and in perfect condition, looked as if he had been sitting on the bench for an hour. His blue-gray baseball suit with WEST POINT across its front was hardly wrinkled.

Omar Bradley was light for an athlete, but he had a well-built frame. His shoulders carried the hint of success on future athletic fields.

Sammy Strang began the business of plunking the baseballs at his feet into a leather handbag. He said, "Bradley, what did they call you at home? Abraham Lincoln?"

Omar laughed softly as he squinted at the coach. "No, sir," he said. "Nothing like that. The boys I played ball with called me Brad." Omar had such a pleasant voice that people liked to hear him talk.

"Well, you look like Lincoln," the coach said. "And I think you've played a lot of baseball. Right?"

"Yes, sir. When I was fifteen, starting high school in Higbee, Missouri, I played on the team. In the summertime we fellows met at the diamond at nine and played till noon. After that we walked two miles and went swimmin'. Then we played ball until suppertime, and if it was a nice evening, we played until dark."

"Who coached you?"

"Sir, we coached ourselves."

"Higbee, Missouri," Sammy Strang said. "Humph! I read over the baseball record cards this morning. Higbee doesn't sound right."

Sammy Strang pulled a handful of white cards from his bag and shuffled them.

"Well, sir," Omar said, "I played three years on the Moberly High team in Missouri. After Dad died, Mother and I moved there."

"Here's your baseball record," the coach said.

OMAR NELSON BRADLEY

Class of 1915

BORN: Clark, Mo., Feb. 12, 1893   POSITION: outfield

PLAYED AT: Moberly, Mo.   BATS: right,

WEIGHT: 148 lbs.   throws right

REMARKS: Captain of his team   HEIGHT: 6 ft.

He wrote on the card: "Hits curve. Fine arm."

"I kept you here," Sammy Strang said, " 'cause I'm sure you can help our team."

Omar's strong face broke into a grin. This was recognition he relished.

"That throw," the coach went on, "from back near those tennis courts was one of the longest I've seen here. Let me see your arm."

Omar rolled up his undershirt. His arm had muscles like those of a 200-pounder.

"How did you get that muscle?" Strang asked.

10

Young Omar Bradley with his mother and father

"Sir, I got this unloading forty-ton railroad cars with a shovel." His quiet midwestern twang emphasized "shovel" with a slightly higher note.

"How come?"

"Sir, after Dad died, there was just Mother and me. I got a summer job on the Wabash Railroad to help with expenses. I swung a shovel ten hours a day, six days a week, at thirteen cents an hour. Last summer I got a better job in a boiler shop at seventeen cents an hour. Both jobs strengthened my arms."

"I know that work made you realize the value of an education," the coach said. "How did you get in here?"

"Sir, our Sunday School superintendent, Mr. Crewson, suggested I apply for West Point. I wrote our Congressman, Mr. Rucker, and he gave me an alternate appointment. When the fellow who had the principal appointment failed, I got in."

"What kind of a student are you? You have to pass each of your studies if you are going to play ball here."

"I'm just a fair student," Omar answered, "but on the entrance exam I found I could puzzle out math. I know I'll have to study hard, because I've been out of school for a year."

"What made you want to come here?" Sammy Strang asked.

"Sir, I came here because I like history, and I knew I could get a fine education free."

The coach stood up and so did Omar. "I'm glad to know you, Brad." The coach shook Bradley's hand. Sammy Strang's hawk-like nose bent a bit when he smiled. "I'm marking you down for the varsity baseball squad next spring," he continued. "You'll be notified to report to me in the gym in mid-February. Keep your eye on left field. And remember this..." Strang paused. "Your opportunity at the Point is bigger than baseball. I hope you'll take advantage of it."

"I aim to," Omar said.

Cadet Bradley sprinted the 400 yards to barracks. He was so happy he felt his spikes were hardly touching the ground.

During the short march to the parade ground in full dress uniform with the other plebes, Omar hardly heard an upperclassman telling him to hold his shoulders back.

When the saluting gun roared, sending its echoes rumbling through the Highlands, a cadet captain in front of the cadets commanded, "Present—*arms!*"

Two hundred and sixty-three plebe rifles snapped to the present position, making a sound as if a hundred teamsters had cracked their whips. The band at the right of the line played the National Anthem. Men, women, and children watching the parade from the iron benches in front of the Superintendent's home stood up.

At Trophy Point enlisted men of the guard pulled the flag down slowly. They guided it carefully through the elms. The cadets at attention in ranks could not see it, for their eyes looked straight to the front.

It was a sacred moment, and each boy stood alone with his thoughts. Omar Bradley, the boy who looked like Abraham Lincoln, decided he would follow that flag forever. If he took advantage of the opportunity the coach spoke about, he could devote his life to his country.

2. Plebe in F Company

Late in the summer of 1911, the plebes of F Company received shooting instruction on the West Point range near the Hudson River. The row of targets, 600 yards away, looked like a line of matchboxes. The sixteen-inch black bull's-eyes were like pencil dots.

A fishtail wind bothered the shooters. Cadet Bradley, in the prone position, waited until the wind blew toward the river. He held his breath, squeezed the trigger, and sent a shot cracking down the range. The bark of the cadets' rifles sounded like the noise of battle.

Down went Bradley's target. He readied his pencil above his score book to note the result, and in a moment the target ran back up. A white disk covered the bull's-eye, signaling that the bullet had pierced the center of the target.

A captain helping to instruct the cadets walked up behind Omar. "Good work, Mister Bradley," he said. "You've handled a firearm before."

Bradley, who had finished his string of ten shots, scrambled quickly to his feet. "Yes, sir, I've had a little experience," he said.

"Where? With what kind of guns?" the officer asked.

"Back in Missouri, sir. Dad bought me a twenty-two when I was seven. He gave me a shotgun the day I was thirteen."

Omar's eyes brightened at the memory. When he was thirteen—that birthday coincided with Lincoln's ninety-seventh birthday—his father took him hunting. He walked down the rows of crisp cornstalks, new gun at the ready. He and his father lacked the help of a dog. When the birds zoomed into flight the shooters had to be quick. The drum-like whirr of the quail bothered Omar at first. "Don't mind that," his father had encouraged. "It upsets everyone at first." Slowly Omar improved and became an amazingly accurate shot.

Nothing worried Omar that plebe summer. The drills and parades on the Plain and problems in infantry tactics calling for hiking in the wooded West Point hills did not tire him. He could see the humorous side of a plebe's life. He realized that the upper-classmen, in their demanding way, were training the plebe class in discipline, neatness, precision, and posture. When upperclassmen yelled at him, Omar Bradley refused to become upset. He told his roommate, Benjamin Mills, "We've got to play this like a game." It was splendid thinking, for new cadets who fretted about the "plebe system" had a far harder time.

Near the end of the summer the F Company plebes sat under the oaks near the hotel at Trophy Point. They listened to a doctor from the Cadet Hospital give instructions on first aid.

When the doctor called, "Take a break!" a first classman took Omar aside. "I hear that you're an outfielder, Mr. Bradley. Right?"

"Yes, sir."

The upperclassman said, "I guess you'll sit on the bench for we have three veteran outfielders, all first classmen. You ought to learn a lot just by watching."

"Watching them?" Omar thought. He remembered Sammy Strang saying, "Keep your eye on left field!" What had he meant by that?

After supper Omar met his two best friends in "plebe heaven"—the top floor of F Company. "Honest John" Leonard perched on the iron banister. Jo Hunt Reaney, of Eugene, Oregon, stood imitating an upperclassman—gray dress coat open, cap on the back of his head.

Omar told them, in his best offhand manner, what the upperclassman had said.

Honest John Leonard, himself a ball player in his home town of Toledo, Ohio, listened carefully. Baseball meant as much to him as it did to Omar.

When Omar finished, Honest John said, "I'm betting on you anyhow. How good are their throwing arms? I wish I could hit a curve like you, Brad. How do you do it?"

"Why," Omar drawled, "I just watch it and if it twists just a little I lead it, just like you do a bird. I aim ahead to meet the ball. If I can help you learn, I'll be glad to do it."

Jo Hunt said, "About that kill-joy first classman. You've got to meet the challenge on the diamond, not in a first aid class." With that Reaney grabbed Omar and tried to wrestle him to the floor. If there was anything Jo Hunt liked, it was a roughhouse.

The three friends enjoyed hiking near Fort Putnam, a Revolutionary War stronghold. On these hikes they liked to think they were mountain climbers.

When studies began in the fall, Omar concentrated for all he was worth. The year he had remained out of school handicapped him at first. He found himself in competition with other boys, some of whom had received special study in prep schools. Also, he was not used to the West Point method of standing beside a blackboard to recite on the work he had written there.

An instructor explained this procedure to his class. "We are training you to make decisions," he said. "The more conclusions you have arrived at, the better. Someday you'll be in a position where you have to make decisions quickly. Lives of men will depend on your judgment, and your decisions will mean much to our country."

This made Omar work harder than ever, for he had a driving urge to succeed.

After about a month Omar felt at ease in the classrooms. His hardest subject was English, his easiest, math. He had no trouble with the Tactical Officers, who were in charge of the discipline. His training at home helped again, for he had learned to obey his parents.

One of the things Omar enjoyed most was being in F Company. He felt as if the 100 cadets were a band of brothers. "One reason for this," he said later, "was the wonderful spirit we had. It began with the football players, who were close friends. We plebes had to mind our p's and q's, but we were F Company plebes. Upperclassmen from other companies did not bother us."

One of Omar's friends in the company was a jaunty plebe with a wonderful grin, Dwight Eisenhower, called "Ike" by his friends. Back in Abilene, Kansas, Ike had also worked hard. Wrestling milk cans into wagons and hustling 300-pound cakes of ice had given him tough muscles and a strong body.

Eisenhower played halfback on the "Cullum Hall team." These were the scrubs, who took a daily pounding in front of Cullum Hall from the heavier varsity. Omar liked to watch them.

The days were warm, yet the smell of autumn filled the air. The design of the gray stone buildings and the guns at Trophy Point made one feel as if he were inside a fort. High on the hill was the crown— the new Cadet Chapel.

After one grueling practice, Omar walked to the gym with Ike Eisenhower. Walking with Ike was like walking with a knight who was leaving the tournament field.

"I admire the fast start you get on those hand-offs from the quarterback," Omar said. "I watched while you practiced getting off the mark on the track last summer."

"You have to be quick," Ike said, "if you want to survive."

"I know," Omar said. "I told the coach I wanted to come out for the squad, but he said I was too light — to see him next year. I'm disappointed."

Two months later the Army-Navy football game was held in Philadelphia. Omar was proud when he marched with the Corps onto Franklin Field, while the West Point band played *Columbia the Gem of the Ocean*. The Navy's cheers, hurled across the gridiron, were deafening. "We don't even have a mule!" moaned the cadet standing at Omar's side.

The Army cheerleaders called for a song. The cadets responded:

"The Army's coming down the river—the river,
The Army's got the goods today.
The Navy goat begins to shiver, and quiver,
When the Army mule begins to bray—
HEE-HAW
When the Army mule begins to bray."

The game seemed as cold as the weather, for Navy won 3-0. At the end, the cadets in the stands removed their caps in honor of their hard-fighting team. The midshipmen poured across the field, and the gridiron became a sea of blue. The sailors pulled off their white-topped caps and sang their new song, *Anchors Aweigh*. Something about that song and the defeat of his team made Omar determined to play on a winning team against the Navy.

3. Batter Up!

The crack of bats on the main floor of the Cadet Gymnasium sounded like explosions of small cannons. Omar waited patiently for his turn to step into the nets of the batting cage. He had never batted indoors before.

The pitcher sent a fast one zipping behind Bill Harrison, the batter.

"Whoa!" yelled Sammy Strang. "You've got to throw them in the strike zone! Next pitcher!"

Harrison met the ball without trouble. He sent six balls whistling back to the pitcher. Next, Ulloa of Costa Rica almost tore the cover off the ball.

Leland Hobbs, a stocky plebe standing in line behind Omar, whispered softly, "Brad, every other guy here's an outfielder." Hobbs grasped the net and leaned on it.

"Take your hands off that net!" Sammy Strang howled. "Me and the gym crew spent the morning hanging these nets, and we don't want anybody leaning on 'em."

Ike Eisenhower lifted the net, tapped the plate with his bat, and met the ball smartly. But Sammy Strang said, "You cadet from Kansas! I'd like to see you quit chopping at the ball!"

When Omar's turn came, he stood well back in the box. His smooth-soled gym shoes felt strange, and he missed the comfort of sinking his spikes into clay.

Omar swung and missed. He expected Sammy Strang to say something, but the coach kept quiet. Omar fouled a half-dozen pitches, then stepped out of the cage to give the next batter his chance.

Sammy Strang motioned Bradley aside. "Now, Bradley," he said, "this is the first time you ever batted indoors. Right?"

"Yes, sir."

"Well, you'll get the hang of it. Don't change your swing to meet the ball. Keep swinging long and loose."

When the practice session ended, the cadets wrapped themselves in their long gray overcoats and jogged through the snow to their rooms. Ike

Eisenhower was beside Bradley. "I read in the paper that the Navy team is practicing outdoors," Ike said.

"It'll be a big day for me, too, when we're on the diamond," Omar said. "I'm progressing backward in that net."

When the season opened against Rutgers University, Sammy Strang had his three veteran outfielders in the lineup. Omar sat huddled on the bench next to Leland Hobbs. The prospects of getting into the game seemed as cold as the north wind whistling between the hills and sweeping the Hudson River.

West Point's 1915 baseball team. Omar Bradley is second from left; Coach Sammy Strang, right.

Eisenhower had been dropped from the baseball squad before the first game. As the season progressed the new players learned that Sammy Strang used few substitutes. He had a winning combination and saw no reason to change it. Omar was disappointed, but he complained to no one.

Suddenly one day Sammy Strang gave Omar a chance in left field. Omar was determined to make good as he trotted to his position. Near the end of the game three opposing runners got on base. It was important that they not score. The batter lifted a lazy fly to left. Omar drifted back, caught it, and threw with all his might. The ball sailed over the catcher's head. After the game an officer said to Strang, "Mr. Bradley has a wonderful arm."

"Wonderful!" Sammy Strang gasped. "Three runs scored on his overthrow!"

"Come here, Bradley," Sammy Strang said the next day. "Go out there in left field and practice throwing home on the first bounce. The catcher can handle it better, and he doesn't have time to run for a stepladder!"

Richards Vidmer, the Army bat boy, was an officer's son. Omar Bradley took time to make friends with Dick and to play catch with him.

It was the dream of every cadet to play against Navy. When the cadet team traveled to Annapolis, they left the train at Baltimore and boarded a special interurban street car. It whizzed along at 20 miles an hour. Omar hoped Sammy Strang would change the lineup, because he felt he could hit any pitcher the Navy placed on the mound.

Sammy Strang rose from his seat in the front of the car. "I'm going to show you," he said to his squad, "what you're up against. Tomorrow we'll meet a pack of howling middies. They'll place a cheerleader in front of our dugout. He'll go like this." Sammy crouched in the aisle. Then he jumped into the air, snatched off his cap, and shouted, "'Four-N Yell' for the team!" He cupped his hands about his mouth and shouted, "N-N-N-N — A-A-A-A — V-V-V-V — Y-Y-Y-Y. NAY-VEE! NAY-VEE! NAY-VEE! TEAM! TEAM! TEAM!" The portly coach gulped for air. "I'm not worried about the Navy's pitching," he said. "I'm worried for fear you fellows will curl up when you hear the middies yell at you."

The cadets laughed long and loud. Sammy Strang was amusing off the diamond, dead serious on it.

In Annapolis the West Point party changed from the interurban to horse-drawn surreys. When the five carriages pulled into the beautiful grounds of the United States Naval Academy, the cadets found the Brigade of Midshipmen lined up on each side of the street in a gesture of welcome.

At the end of the long lane, the cadets jumped to the ground. The midshipmen broke ranks and surrounded them. A cheerleader led a yell for "the Army team." Then thunder broke loose, and the midshipmen roared their famous "Four-N Yell" for their own team. "Don't they do that nicely?" Sammy Strang asked.

Bradley again sat out the game on the bench. But when Army won 7 to 1, he felt rewarded by being part of a winning team.

On the return trip Sammy Strang plunked into a seat beside Omar. "At first blush, Brad," the coach said, "it looks like you wasted time this season. But this year you've just been learning. Next year I'm counting on you to be my regular left fielder."

Omar's long face cracked into a grin. "I can hit," he said.

"I know it. You can also throw, and you'll be bigger and stronger next season." Sammy Strang always had to have the last word.

The coach was right about Omar's weight. By the end of the summer Omar weighed 175 pounds—enough to make him hope he would be considered for the football team.

4. Gridiron War

On the first day of the 1912 football season, Cadet Bradley knocked on the door of the coaches' office in the Cadet Gymnasium.

A voice said, "Come in."

Omar entered, stood at attention before the head coach, and saluted.

Army's head coach, Pot Graves, was sitting at a desk dressed for practice. "Well, what is it?" Graves asked.

"Sir, I want to play football." Omar held his breath, awaiting the answer.

The giant in football uniform stood up. "Any experience?"

"No, sir, but I think I can play."

"Well, that's half the battle. What position?"

"Sir, I want to try out for center."

"How much do you weigh?" the coach asked.

"One hundred and seventy-five pounds, sir."

Lieutenant Graves said, "I think you can pass the ball. I've seen you play baseball. Go to the storeroom and tell 'em I said to issue you equipment. Then report to the Cullum Hall squad."

"Thank you, sir," Omar said.

One of the best players on the Cullum Hall squad was his friend Jo Hunt Reaney. Each evening they returned from the football war, tired but happy.

Playing football made it hard to stay awake and study after supper. Omar had learned good study habits, but football caused his marks to slump. He now stood just below the top 30 per cent of his class.

He liked the cadets on the squad. He liked centering the ball, too, and then the dash through the line, sacrificing himself to help the ball carrier forward. He learned that victory comes from teamwork and slavish hard effort.

Bradley became known to the coaches and the squad as a "team player." He contributed to the varsity's success by scrimmaging against it almost every afternoon. When the Army team improved, Omar was happy. When it suffered defeat, as it did against Navy in a 6 to 0 contest, he felt miserable.

In late February, 1913, the Cadet *Daily Bulletin* carried a special announcement. It said, "The Cadet Baseball Squad will report to Mr. Sam Strang Nicklin on the second floor of the gymnasium at 3:30 P.M. today." Omar's eyes danced.

He now enjoyed batting in the indoor cage. It did not seem as strange as it had the year before.

That season Sammy Strang put together another strong team, and his regular left fielder was Cadet Bradley. Army's hopes trembled before the Navy game, even though the Army's record stood at thirteen games won and five lost. Otis Sadtler, star second baseman and team captain, had sprained his ankle. Bad luck dogged the team. During practice two nights before the game, a grounder took a bad hop and broke the nose of the substitute second baseman, Francis Dunigan. Trainers rushed Dunigan to the hospital. A doctor set the battered nose and placed it in a cast so Dunigan could play in the game.

The next day when Dunigan trotted to the diamond, both of his eyes were black.

"Holy smoke!" Sammy Strang said. "You look like you've been in a prize fight."

"I'm worried," Dunigan said. "The sun's glare on this cast makes it hard for me to see."

Sammy Strang turned to the groundskeeper. "Get me some green paint," Strang shouted.

When the coach finished painting the cast, he stepped back to admire his work. "You look like a green hornet," he laughed. "I know we'll win now! You'll scare the Navy to death!"

About 4,000 fans filled the stands an hour before game time. The Corps sat in bleachers behind the Army bench. Ike Eisenhower, now a cheerleader, called for a "Long Corps Yell" for the team. Then the West Point band blared Army fight songs.

After the conference at home plate with the two big league umpires assigned to the game, Sammy Strang trotted to the Army bench. "Gather 'round me," he said to the players. "I got a phone call from a friend, a big league scout. He said, 'Watch out for this Navy pitcher, Vinson! He's got a good move to first.' When you get on first base, be alert or he'll pick you off. He's quick."

The cadet players sprinted to their positions on the field. The head umpire shouted, "Batter up!"

It was a fast game. Bob Neyland, star cadet pitcher, was as effective as the Navy's hurler. In the last of the ninth the score stood 1-1. Omar Bradley selected his bat from the rack.

"Get on that base!" Sammy Strang commanded.

Omar was in no hurry at the plate. He watched each pitch with a hawk's eye.

"Ball four!" the umpire announced.

The Corps shouted. This could be the winning run.

When Omar got on first, he took his lead carefully. From the coaching box Cadet Sadtler called, "Brad!" Omar looked at him. At that moment the Navy pitcher threw to first. Omar slid back to the base, but the umpire signaled "Out!"

Bradley was angry. He was angry at Sadtler for calling his name, angry at himself for looking, and angry at the umpire. Omar dusted himself off and walked slowly back to the bench. Sammy Strang said nothing. For over 50 years that play rankled Omar Bradley. He believed the umpire had called the play wrongly.

Up to the bat walked the green-masked Dunigan. He surprised everyone by spanking the ball through the diamond for a hit.

"Now don't *you* get picked off!" Sammy shouted.

Cadet Lil Lyman, star batter, sent the ball on a line to deep left center, and Dunigan scampered home with the winning run. Omar was exuberant as he ran off the field.

The next day he examined his railroad ticket when he was back in his room. Each cadet in the class was receiving a 90-day vacation. Two years had passed since he had seen his mother and friends in Moberly. There was a pretty girl there, Mary Quayle, whom Omar knew slightly.

"I hope she'll go out with me," Omar said to his roommate. "We went to high school together."

5. At Battle Monument — West Point

Mary and Omar had been members of the 1910 graduating class at Moberly High School, and Mrs. Quayle had been Omar's Sunday School teacher. Upon his return Omar was welcomed at the Quayle home.

In that summer of 1913, he saw as much of Mary as he could. They went on picnics, and Mary came to see Omar play baseball on the Moberly town team. The summer rushed by. Omar felt lonely as he walked to the Quayle home for the last time before returning to West Point.

"I'll see you again, Mary," he said, "but I won't be home till I graduate. That's two years."

"We can write," Mary said, "and the time will fly by. You'll be playing baseball and football."

When Omar returned to the Academy he found that there was a new cadet in the Corps who was a sensation on the football field. He played center.

After the first day of practice, Jo Hunt Reaney said to Brad, "Did you see that big plebe from A Company, John J. McEwan? He's some sort of genius. He can spout Browning and Shakespeare by the yard, and he starred on the University of Minnesota football team. They call him 'The Giant from Minnesota.'"

Omar scrimmaged almost every day as center on the third team. He was playing well, but his dream of playing football against Navy seemed as dark as cadet barracks after "Taps." That season Omar "owned" a seat on the Army bench.

The following June, Omar and his classmates became first classmen; some became officers in the Corps of Cadets. On his sleeve Omar wore the chevrons and diamonds of a first sergeant.

A Tactical Officer took Omar into his office and explained his duties. "You'll catch on to the work quickly, Mr. Bradley," the Tac said. He opened a ledger. "I checked your demerit record. I have here most of the things you were reported for. You haven't gotten into any trouble at all—it's amazing!"

Omar scanned the list of demerits he had received:

4TH CLASS YEAR

	Punishment
Knocking off full dress hat at parade.	2 demerits
Twice misspelling the word "guard" in written explanations	1 demerit
Collar not adjusted at dinner formation.	1 demerit
Out of bed after Taps.	1 demerit

3RD CLASS YEAR

Long hair at inspection.	2 demerits
Floor not properly swept.	1 demerit
Buckskin gloves not folded properly at morning inspection.	1 demerit

2ND CLASS YEAR

Dust under radiator of room.	1 demerit
Floor not properly swept at morning inspection.	2 demerits

1ST CLASS YEAR

Desk drawer open during parade.	1 demerit
Spurs not properly cleaned at Saturday morning inspection.	2 demerits

"Every officer knows of your ability to carry out your duties," the Tac said. "I'm very sorry you were not appointed a cadet captain."

"Sir," Bradley said, "if it would mean leaving my

company, I would rather be first sergeant in F Company than captain of any other company."

The cadets of F Company howled when they learned this. They teased cadets in other companies about it. Omar had added to F Company's prestige.

It was about this time that Ike Eisenhower wrote the following about Omar Bradley for the yearbook, the *Howitzer*:

> "...Omar Bradley's great passions are baseball, football, F Company, in this order of rank....His baseball batting average is .383.
>
> "...His most prominent characteristic is "getting there," and if he keeps up the clip he's started, some of us will some day be bragging to our grandchildren, "Sure, General Bradley was a classmate of mine."

In the fall the battles on the gridiron continued. Navy was proud of its team. "We're underdogs," midshipmen said, "for we've lost two games. Watch out Army! Underdogs usually win Army-Navy games."

The Corps of Cadets gave its team a noisy send-off as it left by train for the big game in Philadelphia. The Corps would follow the next day. Cadet "Snoops"

Goodman, the second string center, did not make the trip. He had violated a regulation, so the Commandant of Cadets quickly ruled, "Cadet Goodman will walk the area of barracks as punishment. He will not play against Navy."

Charley Daly, who was now head coach, reacted just as quickly. "Bradley," he snapped, "I want you to be prepared! Anything can happen to the first string."

When Cadet John McEwan pulled on his uniform in the Army dressing room before the game, his shoulder pads emphasized his height and strength. He was one of the great centers of football and Omar, his substitute, admired him.

It was a bright Indian summer day in Philadelphia, but the dim lights in the Army dressing room made the room seem like a cave. Coach Daly paced the floor nervously.

A cadet manager opened the door and walked in. "Sir," he said to Coach Daly, "the midshipmen are marching onto the field."

"Never mind the Navy!" Daly snapped. He looked at his watch for the twentieth time. He shouted, "First classmen on your feet!"

Twelve first classmen lined up before Daly. Omar stood at the end of the line.

"It's 'Never again' for you," Coach Daly said to

the seniors. "Lead us to victory!" His blue-gray eyes
flashed. "The rest of you," he shouted, "stand up!
Remember, we *can* beat Navy!"

When the squad dashed out of the dressing room,
the noise of the crowd sounded like a tremendous
train roaring through a tunnel. The Corps sang *On
Brave Old Army Team* at the top of its lungs.

When the game started, Omar sat on the bench, and
the "Giant from Minnesota" started to play his best.
The players wore no numbers, but close followers
of the West Point team had no trouble spotting
John McEwan.

The game was rough. Suddenly McEwan collapsed.
A West Point doctor and trainer sprinted onto the
field. They assisted the giant to the sidelines. "He has
a head injury," the doctor told Lieutenant Daly.

"Bradley!" Daly shouted. "Go in for McEwan!"

It was a crucial substitution because center is a
key position.

In 1914 football players played both offense and
defense. Omar's passes to his backs were perfect,
and he moved quickly to block for the ball carriers.
When the Navy had the ball, Omar backed up the
line, his powerful arms and shoulders nailing the

blue-jersey backs time and again at the line of scrimmage.

Before the final whistle, Omar had substituted twice for the injured McEwan, and Army had dominated the game. The scoreboard read: ARMY 20, NAVY 0.

There was wild excitement in the Army dressing room. The players stood at attention and gave a "Long Corps Yell" for the coaches. It was a great moment for Bradley, because he had seized his chance and had succeeded.

Walter Camp, dean of American football, selected John McEwan as center on his famous All-America team. McEwan immediately turned this into a joke. He said, "Camp thought I was Omar Bradley, so Omar made me All-American!"

In the spring of 1915 the days slid by for Omar and his classmates. Tailors delivered new olive drab uniforms that the first classmen would wear after graduation, when they would all become second lieutenants in the Army.

News of the great war in Europe filled the papers. The question in every cadet's mind was, "Do you think the United States will get into the war?"

In early May, a German submarine torpedoed the British liner *Lusitania*. One hundred and twenty-four Americans went down with the ship.

The New York Times published photos titled "Burying the *Lusitania's* Dead. Funeral Procession in the Queenstown, Ireland Cemetery." The sad pictures made war seem just around the corner.

The first classmen had long discussions with each other and with the Tacs about what branch of the army to choose. Omar and his friends John Leonard, Jo Hunt Reaney, Dwight Eisenhower, and others chose the infantry. Years later when Omar was asked why he chose this hazardous combat branch, he said, "I wanted it because it would give me a chance to lead men in the front rank."

During June Week the Navy baseball team arrived at West Point. The Corps lined the stone wall near the headquarters building and cheered the midshipmen. That evening as the Corps marched to supper, Ike Eisenhower, head cheerleader, hopped out of ranks and led a cheer for the Navy team. In the dining hall the cadets cheered each of their own players.

The next afternoon a funny feeling went through Omar, because he was heading toward the West Point diamond as a player for the last time.

The two teams warmed up while the West Point band serenaded them. Two sailors in blue, from the battleship *Arkansas,* appeared with a goat and led him around the infield. Sammy Strang said, "That goat missed second base!"

In the bottom of the eighth the scoreboard read:

NAVY 0 0 4 0 0 0 1 0

ARMY 2 0 2 2 0 0 0 0

When the last Navy batter lifted a fly to Cadet Leland Hobbs in right field, Hobbs caught it. The Corps howled and snake danced around the infield.

Bradley raced to the bench to shake Sammy Strang's hand. It was a delirious feeling to be a winner. But Omar felt sad as he pushed through the crowd toward the cadet gymnasium for the last time.

In his room he took off his gray dress coat, relaxed in his Windsor chair, and put his feet on the table. He re-read Mary Quayle's "good luck letter." She was now a junior at the University of Missouri, and they planned to be married as soon as she graduated.

A few days later the Class of 1915 fell into ranks for its last formation. It was a perfect day in June. White clouds, floating in a blue sky, peeped over Crow's Nest on Storm King Mountain. A bugler sounded "Assembly." The band and the Colors led the procession to Battle Monument. The cadets, wearing their full dress coats and white trousers, marched their best. It was a gay occasion with sad overtones. Omar hated to say good-bye to his friends, many of whom he would never see again.

When the adjutant called the names of the graduating class, the cadets, one by one, saluted the Superintendent and received their diplomas. No one knew it, but West Point was graduating a famous class. Many who left West Point that day would become outstanding leaders in a terrible world war a quarter of a century away: . . . Eisenhower . . . Aurand . . . Larkin . . . Swing . . . McNarney . . . Leonard . . . VanFleet . . . Hubert Harmon . . . Stratemeyer . . . and Omar Bradley.

6. Infantry Officer

Omar Bradley pulled on his uniform at Fort George Wright in western Washington. He walked briskly to the headquarters of the Fourteenth Infantry Regiment. A saber swung from his Sam Browne belt. It was a strange feeling to be starting a career.

When he had signed at the adjutant's desk, he stood erect before the colonel and saluted. "Sir," Omar said, "Second Lieutenant Bradley reports for duty."

One of the officers of the Post was particularly friendly. This was Forrest Harding, who had been a second lieutenant for seven years.

Harding, a learned man, was running a night school for second lieutenants. "I invite you to join the school, Brad," Harding said. Bradley said years later, "I'm thankful for Forrest Harding. He aroused in me a new interest in my profession."

Omar wrote Mary, discussing their future. But fighting in Mexico changed their wedding plans. A revolution broke out between Mexican leaders struggling for power. Fighting occurred along the border just south of the Rio Grande River. There were bandit raids into the United States. When Americans living in border states asked for protection from the bandits, President Woodrow Wilson sent soldiers.

Bradley was ordered to Arizona for duty along the Mexican border. It was hot and dusty there and water was scarce. This was 1916, and newspapers and magazines were carrying stories of the war in Europe. The Allies—the British Empire, France, Italy, and Russia—were hard-pressed. It seemed as if their enemies—the Germans, Austrians, and Turks—might win.

The Allies purchased supplies from the United States. The Germans, determined to stop these shipments, torpedoed American ships crossing the Atlantic. Most Americans believed that the United States might be drawn into the war.

In December, 1916, Lieutenant Bradley went to see his colonel. Omar saluted. "Sir," he said in his mellow drawl, "I came to see you on a very important matter."

"What is it?" the colonel asked.

"Sir, you see," Bradley said, "I'd like time off to get married."

Omar traveled by train to Columbia, Missouri, where the Quayles were now living. The wedding took place in the Christian Church there. After a short honeymoon in Kansas City, the couple took a train for Yuma, Arizona. In almost no time at all, Omar was back on duty along the border.

The Bradleys were happy even though money was scarce. The pay of a first lieutenant was then only $167 a month.

On April 6, 1917, the United States took a fateful step. It declared war on Germany.

Excitement swept the country. Camps sprang up in many places to train soldiers to fight in the war.

Bradley was anxious to go overseas to fight for the United States. But new orders sent him to training camps in Washington and other western states.

In July, 1918, he received a sad letter which read, "Jo Hunt Reaney was killed in France while leading a machine gun company in a battle at the Marne River. The only thing found was his West Point class ring." It seemed impossible that this buoyant friend was dead.

Finally the war ended on November 11, 1918. Millions were thankful and among them were the Bradleys. But Omar was worried. He told Mary, "Since I was not sent to France, I'm afraid I won't get very far in the army."

At Brookings, Bradley headed the ROTC of South Dakota State College. He enjoyed hunting pheasant in the rolling prairie along the Big Sioux River, but even more, he enjoyed teaching. The students were surprised, for they had expected to find their new commandant a stern military man. Instead they discovered a good-natured, patient teacher.

Four years later Bradley received new orders sending him to West Point to instruct the cadets in mathematics. He liked the cadets, but he had to work hard. "I have to stay ahead of these cadets," he told Mary.

Cadet Russell Reeder, one of Bradley's students, returned to his room after a math class in a happy frame of mind.

"What's come over you?" his roommate, Edward McLaughlin asked.

"Our new math teacher is a great guy! His name is Captain Bradley."

"What's so great about him?" McLaughlin asked.

"He helped me to understand the lesson," Reeder said. "I can do the problems. Captain Bradley's got a soft voice and he's patient."

Cadets turned out the lights in their rooms at ten o'clock, when a bugler blew "Taps." That night, just before the sweet notes of the bugle sounded, Cadet Reeder stood on his table and draped a blanket around the ceiling light.

"What the heck are you doing?" Ed Garbisch, his other roommate, asked.

"I need to study my math lesson some more," Reeder said. "With Captain Bradley's help and a lot of hard work, I'm sure I can pass the course."

Two weeks later the mathematics instructors rotated, teaching different sections of cadets. Cadet McLaughlin returned to his room and shouted at his roommates, "Am *I* lucky? I've got Captain Bradley! Tonight I want you to show me how you draped this light."

In December, 1923, a great event took place in the Bradley family—a daughter, Elizabeth, was born. Omar needed more money now. While on leave from the army that summer he went to work on the new bridge the State of New York was building at Bear Mountain. He labored as a steel worker, for $10 a day, on the 1,600 foot spans high above the river.

A few years later he would serve again at West

Point—as a lieutenant colonel in the Tactical Department. Omar liked this duty, and the cadets liked him, even though some were mystified by his manner. Cadet Harvey Fraser of Illinois said, "I can't get over this Omar Bradley! He hands out demerits just as nice as if he were serving apple pie."

After Omar's first tour at West Point he moved to Fort Benning, Georgia. This was an important time in his career, for Omar, now a major, became a student at the Infantry School. It was soon apparent that missing the war in France would not be a handicap to his military career. Senior officers in the school realized that Bradley was an outstanding officer and a serious student. Bradley gained confidence in his own ability as a military leader.

After Infantry School was over, the Bradley family sailed for Hawaii, where they enjoyed the balmy air of the Islands. In the midst of this beautiful Pacific garden, Omar helped train soldiers to fight for the United States.

In the next thirteen years the Bradley family moved six times. Omar was sent to some of the army's top schools, and he also was assigned to teach school. When he joined the staff of the weapons section at Fort Benning as an instructor, student officers responded to his quiet manner of teaching just as happily as the West Point cadets had done.

One day a sergeant said to Bradley, "Sir, I've found a clearing in the piney woods where wild turkeys fly. If you get some of your friends, I'll guarantee you'll shoot some wild turkeys."

A dozen officers, carrying shotguns, tiptoed through the woods an hour before dawn. They lay down on the brown pine needles and waited for the birds to fly in. When daylight filtered through the trees, a flock of turkeys flew into the clearing. Something startled them and they flew away—all but one bird. It ran right through the place where the men lay, but the experts could not fire for fear of hitting each other.

When the hunters returned, Omar told the story. "Darned," he said, "if that turkey didn't outwit the entire weapons section!"

In 1939 Bradley was on duty in Washington, D.C. Alarming reports started to come in from Europe. Hitler, the German dictator, was oppressing the Jews and was preparing Germany for war.

Suddenly on September 1, 1939, Germany's armed forces struck against Poland. Two days later Britain and France joined Poland. The Second World War had begun.

7. Mission to Africa

Omar was now assigned to the office of General George Marshall, Chief of Staff of the United States Army in Washington. Bradley worked long hours, helping Marshall and his staff to build a larger army in case the country were swept into the war. At the end of February, 1941, General Marshall sent for Omar.

"Bradley," the general said in his crisp way, "You are to be commandant of the Infantry School at Fort Benning. I want you to enlarge the enrollment and to set up new courses for the students. Thousands of young men who want to become officers, as well as older regular officers, will report to you. I want them taught methods of modern warfare. Do you have any questions?"

"No, sir."

When the Bradley family arrived at Fort Benning, a pleasant surprise awaited them—Omar had been promoted to brigadier general.

When the news was published, Bradley's classmates thought of the sentence Ike Eisenhower had written long ago for their West Point year book, ". . . some of us will some day be bragging to our children, 'Sure, General Bradley was a classmate of mine.'" He was the first member of the Class of 1915 to be promoted to general.

Fort Benning bustled with activity as new students poured in. Bradley and his family lived in a home set aside for the Fort Benning commandant. Its stately white columns graced an acre of towering oaks.

One Sunday evening the doorbell rang, and General Bradley opened the door.

A young second lieutenant stood stiffly on the threshold. He saluted and said, "Sir, I report for duty as ordered."

Newly-arrived officers were supposed to report to the adjutant. The general realized that this new officer did not know this custom.

"Won't you come in?" General Bradley asked.
"This is Mrs. Bradley."

Soon Mrs. Bradley said, "Supper is ready. We
would like you to have pot luck with us."

After the meal the general said, "Where are you
going to spend the night?"

"I don't know, sir. I have never been here before."

"Our guest room is vacant," General Bradley said.
"We'd like to have you stay there."

"Thank you, sir."

In the morning after they had eaten breakfast,
General Bradley took the young officer to the
adjutant's office. "I hope you learn a lot here,"
Bradley said, "and enjoy your stay. Good day."

Like every officer in the army, Bradley kept in close touch with the war news. The Germans had smashed into Denmark, Norway, parts of France, and other countries. Italy had joined Hitler. No one could be certain what the Russians would do. German planes were bombing English cities. The Japanese wanted to become one of the top world powers. They were friendly with the Germans and Italians.

To help the important Infantry School become a more efficient center for learning, Bradley brought foreign officers to Fort Benning from the war zones to tell the students about the latest war developments.

Suddenly Japan struck without warning against the United States. On Sunday morning December 7, 1941, their carrier planes lashed at the United States Pacific Fleet. The United States and the Japanese were now at war. Germany and Italy declared war against the United States on December 11.

Two months after Pearl Harbor, General Marshall wrote Bradley, "You have the Infantry School well organized. Orders are on the way for you to train an infantry division."

At Camp Claiborne, Louisiana, Bradley set up the organization to instruct 14,000 soldiers. The soldiers were amazed when their new general went over obstacle courses with them.

Four months later General Bradley received

another division to train. This was the Twenty-eighth Infantry Division, National Guardsmen from Pennsylvania. General Marshall told Bradley to "straighten out this division."

The officers and men came from the same towns, and in many cases majors were serving over captains who had been their bosses at home. Sometimes orders were not carried out.

Bradley called a meeting and explained what he was going to do. "I'm going to organize schools," he said, "so you can learn methods of modern warfare. I am transferring many men to other companies so leaders won't call their men by their first names."

Omar was pleased with their reaction. Officers swarmed about him and many said, "This is the best thing that ever happened to us."

One evening Bradley ordered a 25 mile night march so the men could practice hiking in the dark. He himself tramped along with the soldiers. A sergeant next to him had no idea who Bradley was.

The sergeant stumbled over a stone. "Damn the guy who ordered this hike!" the sergeant snapped.

"Yep, they ought to hang him," Omar said.

When the men discovered that General Bradley had said this, they told the story over and over. At this time writers began to refer to him as "the GI's General."

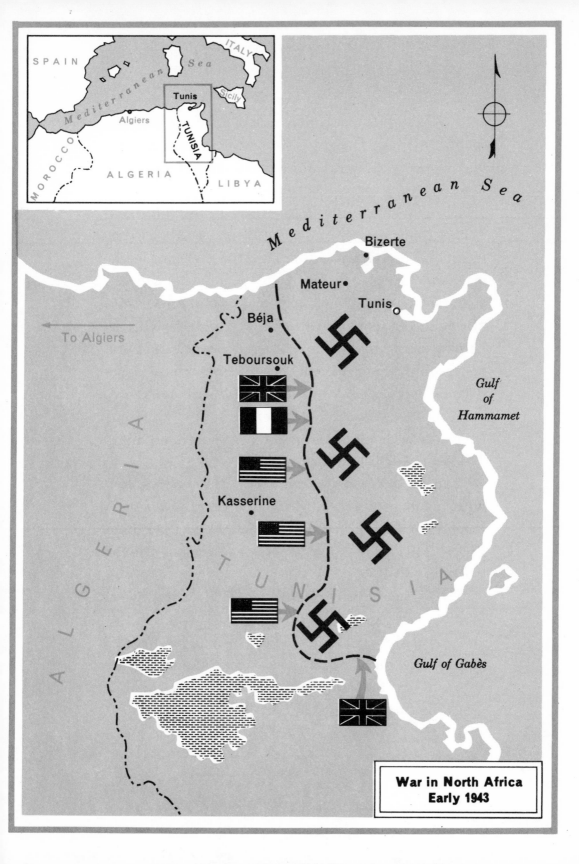

War in North Africa
Early 1943

In early 1943 a conversation in far-off Africa involved Omar. Dwight Eisenhower, now a general, was showing General Marshall a map of the battle lines.

"It isn't easy to pen up the 'Desert Fox,' " Ike said, "but I think we can do it." "Desert Fox" was the nickname for General Rommel, the German leader in North Africa.

Marshall thought a long while and then he said, "Eisenhower, counting the British soldiers who are helping us, our battle line is 280 miles long. In addition, your supply line stretches back 1,200 miles to the Atlantic coast. The Arabs and the French in the area are unsettled. You have dozens of other problems. I have great confidence in you, but you need help."

Eisenhower listened carefully.

"You need a man you can trust," Marshall went on. "You need someone to be your eyes and ears—an experienced leader. Before I fly back to the United States, I'd like to have you select someone for this work."

"Sir," Eisenhower asked, "whom do you have in mind?"

General Marshall pulled a little black book from his pocket. He thumbed its pages and rattled off a few names. Then he said, "What about Omar Bradley?"

"Go no further," Ike said.

8. Fighting Hitler's *Afrika Korps*

Ike Eisenhower was very happy to see Omar Bradley, who flew to Africa and reported to him in Algiers. They had seen little of each other since their days in F Company at West Point.

"Where did you leave your family?" Ike asked.

"Mary is going to live in the Hotel Thayer at West Point," Omar said. "Elizabeth's a young lady now, and she's in college at Vassar."

Soon their conversation turned to war problems. Eisenhower slumped in his chair before a map of Africa. He tapped the easel with a pointer. "We have a tough situation here, Brad," he said. "Our men are spread out over long distances. I want you to get up to the front lines, observe carefully, and then come back and give me your impressions. I'm depending on you."

This was the winter of 1943. Rommel had defeated the Americans and British in a number of attacks, for he had sent his *Afrika Korps* tanks roaring through the dreary Kasserine Pass where the allies had least expected them. Scores of Americans had lost their lives.

In order to carry out his assignment, Bradley rode many miles in a jeep. This was dangerous duty, because the Germans had planted mines, and often their planes would bomb the roads.

One day a lieutenant stopped the general's jeep. "Sir," he said, "the Germans have buried mines here, each made of sixteen sticks of dynamite. When a hidden trip-wire is broken, the dynamite explodes."

The lieutenant led Bradley to one of the mines. Then the lieutenant gasped. "When you drove up, your jeep went over a mine, but the trip-wire didn't work!"

On one visit to the front, General Bradley hiked over the hills toward the enemy. At a lonely spot he met Colonel Kirkpatrick, who had been one of his math students at West Point.

"Colonel Kirkpatrick," Bradley drawled, "do you

realize that there is only a handful of riflemen between you and the Germans?"

"Yes, sir," Kirkpatrick said.

Bradley grinned. "Well, Kirk, good luck! I hope you learned your tactics better than you did your math."

Bradley's reports to Eisenhower, especially those concerning combat leaders, helped in making military decisions.

Soon Ike Eisenhower heard from General Patton. "Sir," Patton said, "I know Omar Bradley's working for you, but I need him. Would it be possible for me to have him as my deputy commander?"

Bradley was pleased when Ike agreed, because he would now have a more vital role in the war.

Bradley and Patton liked each other, and both had a sense of humor. These things served as a bond between them, but they had their differences too. Patton was a showman. He always appeared in a neat uniform of riding breeches, high boots that shone, and a close-fitting jacket. Two large red stars blazed from the front of Patton's car. Bradley gave little attention to dress. It was all right with him if he was unrecognized.

After a month had gone by, General Eisenhower said, "Brad, I am going to give you an even more important job. You will take over Patton's men."

Patton was assigned to help plan the attack against Sicily.

An important thing had happened. Frenchmen, who had resisted the invasion of the Americans and British, were no longer resisting. Some were helping fight the Germans.

Bradley now commanded 100,000 soldiers. He studied the battle front on foot, from the air, and on maps; then he returned to see General Eisenhower. "We can win, Ike," he said, "if you will give me permission to reorganize the battle lines. Our men are too spread out. I want all of the Americans together at the north end of the line, where they can fight as a unit. I also want a definite mission for my soldiers to accomplish."

"U-mmm," Eisenhower mused. "Do you think you can assemble all the American troops in the north? Suppose the Germans found out and attacked while this was going on?"

"I think we can do it," Bradley said firmly.

"What mission do you want?" Ike asked.

"I want orders to seize the high ground leading to Mateur. If we accomplish that, Rommel will be out of luck, for we can then capture Tunis."

"All right," Eisenhower said. "I am trusting you."

Bradley thought it only fair to tell his plans to the newspapermen who were covering the war, so he

invited them to his headquarters. News reporters received such information in advance, and were never known to breach the confidence. When the reporters were seated, Bradley and his aide entered. Omar was carrying the maps, his aide was carrying an easel. The reporters wondered about this, since they had expected the general to make a grand entrance. His uniform puzzled them, for he wore canvas leggings and GI clothing, except for his shoes. He was proud of his shoes, for they had come from Moberly, Missouri, with a stencil on the outside of the uppers which read, "Compliments of the Brown Shoe Co., Moberly, Mo."

Bradley showed his audience exactly how his infantrymen, tanks, and artillery would fight. "We're going to concentrate in the north," Omar said in his soft Missouri voice. "With the help of the British and French, I'm sure we can win."

The reporters were not so sure. Some worried because General Bradley was leaving gaps in the battle line. "What about those spaces, sir?" one asked. "Couldn't the Germans smash through?"

Bradley grinned. "Well," he said, "that's a horse of a different color. If they do, I'll go get another general and some automatic rifles, and we'll battle 'em. But I think the Germans will be too busy up north to have time to attack. The battle line is too long for us to be strong everywhere, so we must concentrate in one area. I think we will win."

One reporter, A.J. Liebling, was impressed with Omar's GI uniform. Liebling wrote, "Bradley is the least dressed-up general in the American army since Zachary Taylor who, in the Mexican War, wore a straw hat."

Rommel, the "Desert Fox," readied the German defenses around Tunis. Hitler had thousands of soldiers and tons of supplies flown in from bases on Sicily.

Bitter fighting broke out on one mountain range after another. The Allies battled their way forward.

The American forces under Bradley fought as a unit. After hard fighting the Germans surrendered. Rommel escaped by flying to Italy. His hard-bitten *Afrika Korps* was defeated and 475,000 soldiers became prisoners of the Allies. Tunis fell into Allied hands.

The Allies had estimated they might capture 200,000 men. General Joe Dillon, in charge of the prisoners, reported to Bradley, "We don't have half enough food, water, medical supplies, or camp sites for this number. What are we going to do?" General Bradley was calm and cool. "Don't worry," he said. "We'll do all we can. Somehow we'll clear up this situation." And they did.

Newsmen had developed great respect for General Bradley, for the battle had been won exactly as he planned. People all over the world wanted to hear about him.

Next the Allies moved across the Mediterranean to invade the island of Sicily. Although the Germans fought hard in the mountainous country, they were slowly driven back. The Italian soldiers, sick of war, surrendered in droves. Bradley led about 80,000 men in this overseas move and attack.

It was late in the second week of the invasion, and the Allies were winning. Major Chester Hansen knocked on the door of Bradley's home-made

Americans (right) fought desperately at Kasserine early in 1943. When the Allies finally defeated the *Afrika Korps* a few months later, almost a half-million German and Italian soldiers surrendered. Nine thousand of these prisoners poured into the camp, shown above, in one day.

trailer. "It's your aide, General," Hansen said. "May I come in?"

"Certainly, Chester," the general said. "What's on your mind?"

"Sir," the young major said, "it's about the writer Ernie Pyle. He wants to write about you." Ernie Pyle, a little, bald-headed newspaperman who came from Indiana, was the most famous correspondent in the war.

Bradley looked over the top of his glasses. "Why," he said, "I thought he specialized in GI's. I don't have time for publicity, and I'm not interested in being written up."

Hansen took a deep breath. "Sir, Pyle puts it this way, 'General Bradley has thousands of men under him, and the parents of those men have a right to know what kind of a guy he is.'"

Omar laughed. "I guess they're entitled to know," he said. "Bring him on."

That same evening the tall general and the short writer climbed into General Bradley's jeep. "Where is your steel helmet, Ernie?" the general asked.

"Steel helmets hurt my head," Pyle said. "That's why I wear this beat-up, olive drab, knitted cap."

"Okay," Omar Bradley said.

Later that night Ernie Pyle wrote, "I like General Bradley because he seems like folks back home."

9. "The Soldiers' General"

Ernie Pyle's articles focused a spotlight on General Bradley. Many war correspondents described his friendliness, his modesty, and his decisions for battle. Pyle also talked of Bradley's humor. Once when Bradley's jeep crawled through a crowd of soldiers, the general had to return salutes constantly.

"I think you need a boy along to return these salutes," Pyle said.

"Oh, this is the way I get my exercise," Bradley answered.

Pyle told of Bradley's jeep driver, Sgt. Alex Stout. Once the sergeant thought Bradley needed a rest, so he drove long miles in the back country pretending he was lost. "The general's working too hard," Stout said. "I had to give him a few hours off."

Pyle wrote, too, of the relationship between the general and the sergeant: "He does everything for me," Stout said. "I go to him for my headaches, advice, and money. He treats me just like my own father does."

Another reporter wrote, "General Bradley talks in a slightly rustic manner. He makes you listen hard for the next phrase."

Because Bradley exposed himself to danger with his men, because he lived simply as they did, and because he was an honest, down-to-earth person, he became known as "The Soldiers' General." The title fitted him perfectly.

After the Americans and British defeated the Germans in Sicily, the Allies readied themselves for new attacks against Germany and her allies. They believed that the quickest way to break Hitler's hold on Europe was to attack the enemy from three directions. The Russians, who had joined the Allies, would continue to fight the Germans in the east. British and American forces would battle their way through Italy. They would soon launch a third attack against the Germans from across the English Channel.

NORWAY

SWEDEN

DENMARK

Baltic Sea

U.S.S.R.

IRELAND

GREAT
BRITAIN

London

NETHERLANDS

BELGIUM

GERMANY

Berlin

POLAND

English Channel

CZECHOSLOVAKIA

Paris

Munich

Vienna

AUSTRIA

HUNGARY

FRANCE

SWITZERLAND

Bordeaux

Marseille

ITALY

YUGOSLAVIA

Adriatic Sea

SPAIN

Madrid

Corsica

Rome

Sardinia

Mediterranean Sea

Sicily

Algiers

Tunis

MOROCCO

ALGERIA

TUNISIA

LIBYA

Allied Invasions of Europe 1943-1944

☐ Allied and freed by Allies

Axis

Axis-occupied

Neutral

General Bradley was checking on his soldiers for the crossing into Italy when a staff officer interrupted. "Sir," the officer said, "this radio message just came for you in code from Washington."

TOP SECRET

From Marshall to Eisenhower, pass to Bradley. The American Army in the Cross Channel attack will be led by General Bradley. He is to fly to Washington immediately for conferences.

Bradley stared at the message. His first reaction was disappointment in leaving his soldiers.

Then there was a brief good-bye to Eisenhower before Bradley's plane droned across the Atlantic. With him flew Chester Hansen.

When the plane taxied to a stop in New York, Omar was surprised to find Mrs. Bradley and Elizabeth.

"How did you know I was coming?" Bradley gasped.

"General Marshall had his secretary call," Mrs. Bradley said.

There was a short but joyful reunion. Elizabeth told her father her exciting news. She would marry Cadet Hal Beukema when he graduated from West Point the following June. "Can you come to the wedding?" Elizabeth asked.

"I won't know until I get back," Omar said.

In the next two weeks Bradley saw President Roosevelt and General Marshall. Bradley also studied secret reports from Europe. They told of hundreds of thousands of men, women, and children who had been torn from their homes and who were forced to work as slaves for Hitler. He and his Nazi political party had returned Europe to the Dark Ages.

Marshall talked forcefully about the invasion of Europe. "We *must* make it succeed!" he said to Bradley. "It has to be a giant step in knocking Germany out of the war." Marshall impressed upon Bradley that his ability to get the cooperation of people everywhere would be a tremendous asset in organizing for the invasion in England. "We have to remain friends with our allies if we're to win," the older general remarked.

When Bradley had selected officers who would join his staff in England, General Marshall said, "Bradley, we can spare you for a week. Take my plane and fly to West Point, visit your family, then fly back here for more conferences. After that—" the older general paused, "—you'll want to fly to England to get ready for the invasion. I wish you Godspeed."

Many important people drove to the airfield to greet Bradley when he arrived in England in October, 1943. American and British air force and army generals watched as Bradley walked down the steps from his plane. High-ranking leaders crowded about him, shaking his hand. In the back rank stood Major Richards Vidmer.

Omar Bradley quickly greeted the generals and rushed over to Vidmer with a big grin. "Why, Dick!" he said. "I didn't know you were here. I haven't seen you since you were a boy taking care of our bats at West Point."

All of England was rapidly becoming an armed camp. Thousands of United States soldiers were arriving by ship. Bradley had the problem of feeding and housing these men. There were other problems, for a U.S. staff sergeant's pay equaled that of a British captain. Bradley told his officers, "Encourage our men to send money home, and also make sure that they understand how these fine people think."

On D-Day—the day of the landings in Normandy—130,000 British and American soldiers would cross the Channel in boats, and 22,000 others would land by parachutes and gliders. Of the total, 72,800 were Americans who would fight under General Bradley.

He checked to make sure they had ammunition, food, clothing, and all of the equipment they needed. In addition, his men would take with them 5,200 vehicles. Those being taken ashore with the first waves of men needed special waterproofing.

General Eisenhower, center, became the supreme
commander of the invasion of Europe. He is shown
here with Generals Bradley, right, and Montgomery.

Bradley said to his division commanders, "I am
especially interested in developing leadership. I
want the young officers to be given responsibility
in maneuvers in order to prepare them for the real
test coming up."

Under Bradley's supervision, soldiers who would
land in Normandy practiced by landing on the British
coast.

When General Bradley arrived in England it had
not been decided who would lead the entire invasion.
A possibility was General Bernard Montgomery.
"Monty" had helped defeat the *Afrika Korps* in

Africa. He was a fine general and a hero to the British people. Bradley respected his ability, but he was not a close friend of the Englishman. Bradley and other Americans felt relieved when they learned that General Eisenhower would head the invasion.

The greatest secret of the Allies was the time and place of the landings. Hitler knew there would be an invasion and he would have given a fortune for detailed information. Brave Allied pilots flew far into Germany to bomb industrial sites. They also bombed the coastline fortifications. It would be hard to guess from all the bombing where the D-Day landings would take place.

In a top-secret conference, General Eisenhower said to Bradley, Montgomery, and other senior leaders, "I am setting D-Day as June 5, 1944. Pass this secret to your top generals first, but by the time our men board their landing craft I want every last man crossing the Channel to know that this is the real thing. It should be no secret to our soldiers and sailors who are going to risk their lives.

"When we land," General Eisenhower continued, "we can expect the Germans to hit us with all their fighting strength. I'm positive we can get ashore, but then we have to break out of the Cotentin Peninsula."

"I'm already working on a plan for that," General Bradley said.

The German defenses were formidable. For four years Hitler's soldiers, helped by slave labor, had been fortifying the 860 mile European coastline. Powerful guns, cased in concrete, guarded the beaches. Machine guns, in steel and concrete pillboxes, were placed so they could spray possible landing places with bullets. Barbed wire and iron posts protected the beaches against landing craft. Just inland, particularly at Utah Beach, the Germans had flooded the lowlands as an additional obstacle.

One day before the invasion, General Eisenhower telephoned. "Brad," he said, "the Prime Minister has an itch to fire the new American carbine. I'm coming with him. Can you set up a place where we can shoot?"

"No problem," Bradley said. "I'll meet you at the headquarters of the Ninth Infantry Division."

When the party arrived Bradley greeted them. He introduced General Manton Eddy, the commander of the division, to Mr. Churchill. General Bradley gave a short talk on the operation of the small rifle, then he handed loaded weapons to Churchill and Eisenhower.

The Prime Minister's eyes twinkled. "I haven't fired a rifle since the Boer War."

"It's really quite easy to fire," Bradley said. "I've arranged for a little competition."

Eisenhower laughed. He said to Churchill, "Sir, I am warning you we are up against one of the best shots in the U.S. Army."

"I don't know about that," Bradley drawled, "but I suggest that Mr. Churchill shoot at that target twenty-five yards away, General Eisenhower will shoot at the one fifty yards away, and I'll take the far one. It's seventy-five yards."

The bullets ping-cracked down the range. When each man had banged off fifteen shots, General Eddy ripped down the targets and hustled away with them.

Churchill laughed. "You Americans! You excel in diplomacy! I don't think I even hit the target."

Bradley then took Churchill and Eisenhower to

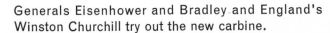

Generals Eisenhower and Bradley and England's Winston Churchill try out the new carbine.

see some training exercises. He wanted to show the Prime Minister that the United States Army was ready for its great challenge across the English Channel.

As D-Day drew near, General Bradley sensed a nervousness among the soldiers. One of his staff officers said, "Sir, all the men are saying good-bye in their letters home. If a spy gets hold of any of the outgoing mail he'll know that D-Day is just around the corner. We are stopping all outgoing mail."

Now the warmth of Omar Bradley's personality and character came through. He drove throughout southeastern England to talk to his soldiers.

"You D-Day men!" he said to them. "You'll be telling your grandchildren about this invasion of the Continent. I do not have to tell you how much we're pinning our hopes and future on you. Over two years of careful planning have gone into this effort. I am entirely confident that we will win. I want no surrender unless you are wounded and are out of ammunition."

His voice now became unusually tense and a bit higher pitched. Each man felt as if the general were talking directly to him. "Remember this: Do not become discouraged, no matter what happens! Continue to fight! More troops are coming in right behind you."

10. Daring Move on the Battlefield

The greatest invasion in the history of man got underway on June 6, 1944, after a delay of one day because of weather.

The mammoth fleet of ships chugged out of bays, harbors, and rivers and assembled off the coast of southern England. As the little boats started across the Channel, they were greeted by stiff winds. The winds swept out of low, lead-gray clouds and served up froth and whitecaps. Gray-green waves banged into each vessel. Many soldiers became seasick. The boats plunged on. Their Navy and Coast Guard crews worked diligently to keep them going.

Yanks, British "Tommies," and "Canucks"—the nickname for Canadians—were ready to land and determined to win.

Barrage balloons floated above many of the boats to ward off possible low-flying German planes. The bad weather gave the Allies an advantage, for the German air force could not attack. German warships also were unable to attack the troop ships because they were guarded by His Majesty's men-o'-war and the United States Navy.

General Montgomery, commanding all the landing armies—under Ike—rode on the destroyer H.M.S. *Faulknor*.

General Bradley stood on the bridge of the cruiser U.S.S. *Augusta* as her prow cut through the waves. Newsmen down in the wardroom of the cruiser talked of the battles ahead. One said, "We're up against Hitler's best general, Rommel. He's the German we have to beat."

"I know it," another said, "but we've got Bradley. I just talked to him. He's confident—calm as a mill pond on Sunday."

"Calm is right," Lieutenant John Mason Brown, of the Navy, said. "Two nights ago we were watching a 'whodunit' movie—Alfred Hitchcock's *Lifeboat*. A call came for General Bradley to report to Ike. Obviously the rotten weather would be the subject, and the invasion might have to be postponed. As General Bradley got up he said to me, 'Brown, will you please tell me later how this movie comes out? And ask them to save me some ice cream, will you?' Bradley could have been back in Moberly, Missouri."

After supper Bradley unbuckled his life preserver and kicked off his shoes in the captain's cabin on the *Augusta*. He crawled into his bed. He *was* calm, but he was tired. He tried to read the paper but gave it up. He read snatches of his wife's last letter. Elizabeth would be married in two days in the Cadet Chapel at West Point. He wanted very much to attend the wedding of his only daughter.

D-Day began for Bradley with abrupt suddenness. At 3:30 A.M. the bell outside his cabin clanged crazily, signaling "General Quarters." Each man on the warship sprinted to his battle station. Omar rushed to the bridge, fastening his steel helmet. Red flashes from a German battery, deep in the Normandy woods, darted at a thousand Royal Air Force bombers flying over the coast. Thousands of American bombers blasted the German defenses. Red and black explosions dotted the coast. Then the beaches looked as they had before the planes appeared—faint gray pencil lines. The bombers had helped subdue the enemy, but the infantry had to go ashore and fight to win.

On D-Day, in Normandy, American infantrymen
plunged ashore to begin the invasion of Europe.

Then the *Augusta* and other men-o'-war swung into
position and started to fire at the German forts. The
noise was deafening. The cruiser shook as if it were
coming apart. After three hours of bombing, swarms
of little landing craft loaded with soldiers sped toward
the beaches.

Hansen read Bradley a message, "Sir, at Utah
Beach, infantrymen are pushing through artillery
fire to join paratroopers who jumped last night."

Thousands of other infantrymen were wading
through the flooded meadows to get inland faster,
because the causeways across the meadows were

now blocked by traffic. Other units were attacking forts along the coast.

Fierce resistance by the Germans stopped the American attack at Omaha Beach. In the afternoon it looked as if the Americans might be pushed back into the sea.

Bradley boarded a fast PT boat and sped to the ship *Ancon*, where other generals were gathered. He ordered them to send reinforcements ashore as soon as it got dark.

Allied Landings in Normandy D-Day, June 6, 1944

The next afternoon Bradley went ashore to Utah Beach. He took Lieutenant John Mason Brown and three war correspondents with him. The party saw the wreckage created by the fighting.

General Bradley stopped at a beach tent hospital and talked to the wounded men and to the doctors. Then he said to his party, "I'm going inland to talk to General Collins. If you want to go back to the *Augusta*, please be here at five."

Lieutenant Brown walked with Bradley to one of the narrow causeways that bridged the flooded area. A jeep chugged by. General Bradley raised his hand and began thumbing a ride.

Lieutenant Brown looked around. "General," he said, "I think I can get you a car or a truck."

"I don't mind a jeep," Omar said.

The driver of a jeep recognized the general and slammed on the brakes. A private first class leaped out. "General Bradley! You can have my seat."

"No, thank you, son," Bradley said. "You look tired. There'll be another jeep along here directly."

Nearby he saw a soldier shivering. General Bradley said, "Take my jacket. I can get another easier than you can."

Later Brown wrote, "The GI's loved him. He was indeed *their* general. He was a master of strategy, and he was one of the most human of men."

More and more Allied soldiers were landed on the beaches. Gradually Rommel's stout defenders were overwhelmed and were pushed inland. Vicious fighting broke out in the hedgerows—rows of rock, bushes, brambles, and trees that marked the borders of the fields. The hedgerows made every field a fort.

Three weeks later Bradley's men had overpowered the Germans, pushed them still farther back, and had captured the port of Cherbourg.

Now came one of the great tests of the war. It was a critical time, for the Allies now had control of the peninsula, but they were penned up in it. How were they going to break out of Normandy?

General Eisenhower was worried. He conferred with General Bradley in a field guarded by the Normandy hedgerows and U.S. soldiers. They studied Omar's huge map which was eight feet long.

"Brad," Eisenhower said, "I'm thinking about the horrible stalemate that developed in France during World War I. Long lines of armies faced each other, while trench warfare dragged on and on."

"Indeed I remember," Bradley said. Then he explained the plan he had worked out in England. "I am sure I can make this work," he said. "I believe it will give us maximum results with minimum loss of life."

After Ike approved Bradley's plan, Omar explained

it to Air Force leaders. "This is the breakout," he said. "I want a bomb carpet 2,500 yards deep by 6,000 yards wide, right in the German lines. You place the carpet here," he said, pointing at the map. "Your bombing will be followed by our tanks and infantry who will rip through the German lines. They'll be followed by more infantry in trucks and jeeps."

"But," one Air Force officer said, "if we do as you suggest we might drop bombs on your soldiers."

"That's why I want you to fly parallel to the road between St. Lo and Periers," Omar said.

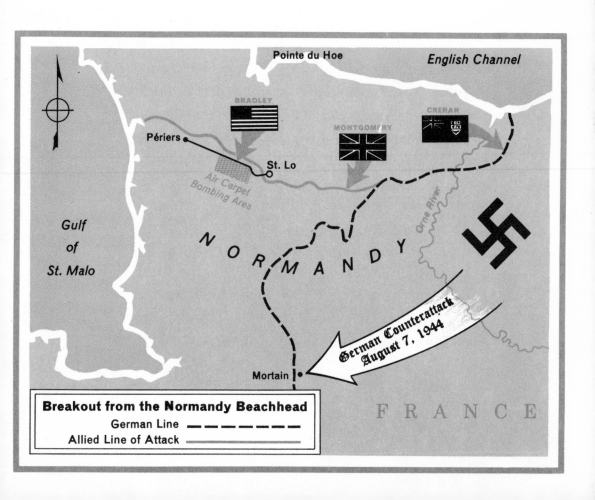

Breakout from the Normandy Beachhead
German Line
Allied Line of Attack

The attack plans were completed, and the Air Force operation was executed. The hole in the German lines was opened as planned. But the bombers flew the wrong way along the road and killed a number of the American soldiers. Omar felt terrible about this mistake.

When the bombing stopped he sent General Collins and over 75,000 of his men through the hole.

Hitler was furious. He sent his best soldiers to Mortain, with orders to crash through the American lines. If they could do this, they would wreck Bradley's plan, and his men who had plunged over the "carpet" and off the peninsula would be cut off.

This was another critical time. The success of the invasion hung in the balance. There were two courses Bradley could follow: he could play it safe, taking no chances, and order his men to abandon the plan of attack through the hole. His forces would then smash back at the Germans attacking at Mortain. *Or* he could be daring and send more soldiers through the hole that had been drilled through the German lines.

Omar checked first on his hard-pressed men at Mortain. They said they could hold the Germans. He believed them.

Next he talked to Patton on a field telephone. "George," he said, "this is the time to take a chance! Push through the hole as hard as you can! Keep

Generals Hodges, left, and Patton, right, share a
moment of relaxation with General Bradley.

those tanks moving. Head for Brittany. I'll see that
supplies reach you."

"I am with you!" Patton said.

This daring decision was followed by successful
action, and the Allies were able to break out of
Normandy. The Germans failed to crash through the
Allied lines at Mortain, and, almost trapped from the
rear by Patton's men, had to retreat.

General Bradley was saddened by the loss of the
lives of many of his men, as he was after every battle.
His planning and leadership labeled him as one of the
best generals in army history. Later Prime Minister
Churchill said, "The choice made by General Bradley
was the most daring decision in the battle for France."

11. Battle of the Bulge

It finally became clear to Hitler that retreat was his only salvation. He ordered his army to withdraw slowly across France, leaving behind 50,000 prisoners and many dead.

A crowd of newspaper reporters called on Bradley. "General," one of them said, "can you arrange it so Paris will be spared? If artillery shells hit it, many beautiful buildings will be ruined."

Bradley smiled. "Our plan is to swing behind Paris and pinch it off. Then we can go into the city when we want to."

"Which division will you send in first?" another reporter asked.

"I don't know," Bradley answered. "There are enough of you newspaper fellows to capture the city by yourselves."

Word had come from the French Underground— French civilians who were fighting the Germans— that Hitler had designated Paris a "fortress." He would defend the beautiful city until, as he put it, "It is a field of ruins."

Bradley knew how much Paris meant to the French. Consequently, after talking with Eisenhower, he changed the plan, sending a spearhead to the city. Bradley issued orders, through military channels, for the French General Jacques Leclerc to enter Paris.

Bradley could have arranged to be the first to enter the French capital. Instead he explained to his staff, "General Leclerc and his men have the honor of entering first. I'll come in later."

But the Germans resisted more than anyone expected. General Bradley then sent soldiers from the United States Fourth Infantry Division to help Leclerc. The gates of the city opened. That evening Paris started its celebration. After four years of occupation by the Germans, the city was free.

About this time, Bradley's men captured a German ice cream machine. Omar found a fifteen-year-old boy from Luxembourg running it. "I want to go all the way to Germany with you," the boy said.

"All right," Bradley answered. "Can you spare a little ice cream for me and my driver?"

While Paris was being liberated and Allied armies were sweeping across France, the Germans were attacked on another front. An Allied army had landed in southern France and was fighting its way north. The Russians were also making progress in Poland as they fought toward Berlin.

The Germans retreated to the shadow of their West Wall. The Allies, since D-Day, had pushed them back over 300 miles. Now the Allied armies bogged down, for their advance across France had been so swift they had run out of supplies. Allied bombing had destroyed many bridges, so the railroads were not running.

In November, 1944, Bradley joined General Eisenhower in his headquarters in the palace of Versailles, just outside Paris, to discuss the situation. A top-secret map hung on the wall. It showed the German West Wall, supposedly the toughest defensive position in the world, and the location of German military units. Many of Hitler's soldiers were living in underground bunkers where Allied guns could not reach them. In addition, numbers of Germans were not in the Wall's defenses but were west of them. They were extremely reluctant to yield any more ground.

General Bradley scans the sky in France for Allied planes. American soldiers, right and below, pursue fleeing Germans through a bombed-out French town and in the countryside.

Snow was now falling, supplies were short, and the outlook for the Allies was dreary. How were they to pierce the Wall?

Ike said, "I tell you, Brad, I've studied this from every possible angle. We need more men if we are going to smash through and crack the West Wall."

"I agree," General Bradley said quietly.

The two leaders decided it would be fatal to sit and do nothing, so Eisenhower ordered an offensive at the northern part of the battle line. The offensive moved the Allies only seven miles, then it was stopped by the Germans and bitter weather.

Omar Bradley worried because many of his men lacked warm clothing and shoe-pacs—boots that would help prevent frostbitten feet. He did everything he could to get cold weather gear to his men.

In a conference with Troy Middleton, one of Bradley's generals, Bradley put his finger on the map and said, "We are stretched thin in the Ardennes, but we can't be strong everywhere. We are taking a calculated risk, but if the Germans smash through here they won't accomplish much."

Bradley and Eisenhower met again near Paris. While they were in conference, a staff officer entered the room. "Sir," he said to General Eisenhower, "we just got a flash. The Germans are counterattacking heavily through the Ardennes, sir."

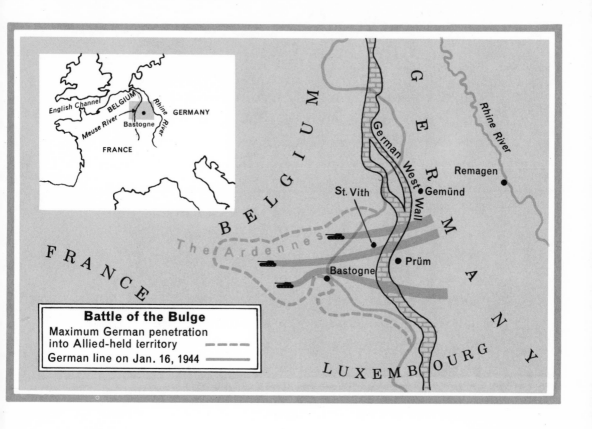

Battle of the Bulge
Maximum German penetration
into Allied-held territory — — — — —
German line on Jan. 16, 1944 —————

Both generals took the news calmly. "What do you think, Brad?" Ike asked.

"I think Hitler's trying to head for ports on the English Channel," Bradley answered. "We can stop him on this line." Omar penciled a line on the map along the Meuse River.

But some newspapermen were not as sure of the outcome of the German drive. They sent alarming reports to the newspapers back home. Many people wondered if the German counterattack would be able to stop the Allies.

It was indeed a serious time. The German drive was a strong one. It seemed as though the drive might split the Allied line at the point where the British and American forces joined. To make sure the Allied forces were coordinated, Bradley flew to talk to General Montgomery. Montgomery's headquarters was north of the "Bulge," as the newspapermen nicknamed the German spearhead.

The sight of Dutch villagers celebrating Christmas made General Bradley miss his family. "But," he thought, "the sooner we stop this German attack, the sooner the war will end."

Bradley was disappointed in his talks with General Montgomery, for it seemed that the British leader was in no hurry to send his troops to fight against the Germans. Montgomery wanted to be sure that the Germans had spent all their strength before he ordered his soldiers to crush forward against the shoulders of the attack. Bradley did not think this wise, for he favored vigorous action as the best course to stop the Germans. He was putting into the fight every man he had.

Some of Bradley's soldiers were now temporarily placed by General Eisenhower under General Montgomery, because they were on Montgomery's side of the German thrust. The British press played this up, picturing Montgomery as "rescuing the shattered American armies." There was also talk in London papers suggesting that Bradley should be placed under Montgomery's control. Montgomery would be "top ground commander," according to the British press.

Bradley went to see General Eisenhower about this. "I don't like it, Ike," Omar said. "It's not true, and it undermines my position with my soldiers. After what has happened I cannot serve under Montgomery."

General Eisenhower seemed impatient.

Bradley said firmly, "If he has to take over all of the Americans, you must send me home."

Ike flushed. He stared at Omar. For a moment it seemed as if their long friendship would end. "Well," Ike said angrily, "I thought you were the one person I could count on! I thought you would do anything I asked."

"You *can* count on me, Ike," Omar said. "I've enjoyed my service with you, but this is one thing I cannot take."

General Eisenhower calmed down, and he and Bradley parted as friends. Some Americans, those on Montgomery's side of the Bulge, would remain under British control until the attack was stopped. Then they would again serve under General Bradley.

The battle line of the Bulge stretched for approximately 165 miles. Americans and the British were now locked in a desperate struggle with Hitler's best soldiers.

At St. Vith and Bastogne, in the center of the push, the Germans fought hard against Americans who also fought hard and refused to surrender. The Germans guessed that Bradley would send reinforcements to rescue the Americans, so the Germans sent men dressed as American officers to misdirect relief expeditions. Some of these German daredevils told a United States military policeman that they were West Point graduates.

The MP was suspicious. He said, "In that case, what was the score of the last Army-Notre Dame football game?" The Germans could not answer that question and other queries, so they were captured.

Reserves—soldiers whom Bradley had placed wisely before the German attack—now entered the fight all along the line. The Germans were stopped short of the Channel ports, along the line Omar had penciled on Ike's map. Hitler's gamble cost him over 250,000 men killed, wounded, or missing.

The Americans, British, and Canadians now faced the problem of getting through the West Wall. Hard-fighting American soldiers finally pierced it west of Prüm and in the Gemünd area farther north. When they explored the Wall, they discovered that the famous defensive system had been weakened

American infantrymen advance cautiously through the burning rubble of a German city.

by Hitler. He had sent many of its big guns to the Channel, spreading them along the coast, hoping to stop the invasion of France.

Hitler, equally concerned about the victories of the Russians, had sent nine divisions from the Wall to the Russian front.

Eisenhower studied the next Allied problem: how to get across the Rhine, for the Germans still held its east banks. The great river had not been crossed by an enemy since the time of Napoleon.

The Germans had blown up bridges over the Rhine as the Americans approached. But they missed one.

In the excitement of fighting toward the river's banks, Omar Bradley suddenly phoned Eisenhower. "I have real news for you, Ike," Omar said. "Our soldiers have seized a bridge across the Rhine at Remagen! It's shaky, but we have it."

Bradley had his engineers repair the bridge, while the Germans fought furiously to prevent them from doing so. Up and down the river temporary bridges were also under construction. Soon Bradley was able to send infantry across, then artillery and tanks — into Germany.

Germany's armed forces now began to collapse. The Allies on the west and the Russians on the east pushed steadily through Germany. They met on April 25, 1945.

In order to keep from being captured, Hitler committed suicide in Berlin. The Germans finally surrendered on May 7, 1945.

The night before the surrender, Omar Bradley wrote a letter to his wife. He told her that he longed to see her and Elizabeth. At Bradley's elbow lay his map case and his helmet now bearing four stars. Only four years before he had started his war career as a one-star general at Fort Benning, Georgia. The man known as "The Soldiers' General" was thankful he had survived and that he had had the opportunity to serve his country in time of need.

12. Five Star General

Crowds thronged to the Moberly, Missouri airport in June, 1945 to give General and Mrs. Bradley a homecoming celebration. Six hundred soldiers, marching to lively band music, led the parade into town. Fighter pilots performed stunts high up in the sky. The Moberly High School band led the Governor of Missouri, Gold Star Mothers, Boy Scouts, Camp Fire Girls, Girl Scouts, Veterans of Foreign Wars, and others in the parade. Omar's high school classmates were guests of honor. Mayor McCormick of Moberly remembered to invite men who had played baseball with Omar Bradley in his boyhood days and at West Point. The happy celebration lasted two days.

President Truman now sent for Bradley. Three months had passed since the end of the terrible war.

"General Bradley," the President said, "I have a job for you. We must take good care of almost three-quarters of a million sick and wounded fighting men. I'd like you to become the head of the Veterans' Administration."

Bradley started his new job. He studied the Administration problems. "About 70 Veterans' hospitals must be built," he said. "Let's put them near medical centers and medical schools, for I want the finest doctors available for patients."

Bradley got things done, although there were arguments with Congressmen, contractors, and veterans' organizations. In his persuasive manner, he was able to convince Congress that his needs were real, and considerable legislation was passed to help returning veterans.

Those soldiers whose education had been interrupted were allocated money to finish school. Veterans who were still ill from the effects of the war were given help, and those with permanent disabilities were assisted.

Although it was a tremendous task, Bradley completed the job to the satisfaction of the President and the country.

In February of 1948 Bradley was promoted to Chief of Staff of the United States Army. Now he would turn again to problems of a military nature.

The new chief was amazed by the small size of the army. "The army is so small it is dissolving in my lap," he told a congressional committee. "We must have more than the present strength of less than 600,000 soldiers to protect our country adequately."

"War is a calamity, and we want to avoid it. But we must be prepared in case of an attack," Bradley said later in a speech. He was successful in getting Congress to appropriate funds to rebuild the army.

It was not long before Bradley became Chairman of the Joint Chiefs of Staff. This is the highest ranking post in the armed forces next to the President, who is the Commander-in-Chief.

In early June, 1950, Bradley's attention focused on the Far East. There North Korean soldiers were crossing into South Korea in raiding parties and were killing the people. Bradley flew to Tokyo and conferred with General Douglas MacArthur. It appeared that the South Koreans could quell these attacks.

But on June 25 over 60,000 North Korean soldiers smashed into South Korea. Aided by Russia, these soldiers had 100 Russian-made tanks and other Russian equipment. The Korean war was on.

The United Nations asked member nations to help stop the invasion, but Russia refused to cooperate. The United States felt responsibility to help stop this aggression. They were to be aided by other United Nations forces.

Omar Bradley was now responsible for soldiers fighting 7,000 miles away. General MacArthur became commander for all United Nations forces in Korea.

General Bradley was opposed to having the war spread, and he was against sending U.N. soldiers across the Thirty-eighth Parallel into North Korea. Bradley told the President, "We must think of the question of China entering the war, for there are storm signals. The Chinese say they will not tolerate foreign aggression. China may defend North Korea if we enter that part of the country. Then Russia might come in and help China. The Chinese and Russians have a treaty to defend each other."

Bradley's advice was respected but disregarded. President Truman gave MacArthur permission to cross the Thirty-eighth Parallel into North Korea on September 29, 1950.

One month later 150,000 Chinese Communists surged across the Yalu River. These were hard fighters, used to hardship and hunger, trained in the guerrilla wars of China. Many more Chinese Communists joined the fighting, and the U.N. army was pushed back to the Thirty-eighth Parallel.

Meanwhile General MacArthur was not in

Both administrator and man of action, General Bradley, right, prepares to testify before a committee of Congress and, below, visits Korea.

agreement with President Truman or with General Bradley. The great general in the Far East believed that U.N. forces should extend the war beyond the borders of North Korea, and that a decisive victory could be won only by bombing targets in Manchuria.

This defiance of civil authority caused Mr. Truman to relieve General MacArthur and to bring him back home. Many Americans were upset by this move.

When a friend asked General Bradley about this he said, "The President of the United States is the Commander-in-Chief under our Constitution. Every member of the Joint Chiefs of Staff recognized that General MacArthur had to be relieved."

The Korean fighting ended on July 27, 1953. A month later Bradley had completed two successive terms as Chairman of the Joint Chiefs of Staff. He entered civilian life and later became chairman of the board of the Bulova Watch Company and director and trustee of many industrial and charitable organizations. Technically he was not retired from the army, since he had become one of the four five-star generals of the United States. He was still available to help the country in time of need. Presidents Eisenhower, Kennedy, and L. B. Johnson have asked for his advice.

People everywhere loved him. They knew he hated war, for he spoke on this subject many times.

On one occasion he marched beside the casket of a soldier who had been killed in action in Germany. Corporal Wilkin had won the Medal of Honor by fighting bravely and by carrying wounded to a first aid station. When he was re-buried near his home at Longmeadow, Massachusetts, in 1948, General Bradley spoke. He told how other young men had defended their homes at Concord in 1775 and in other wars. He said, "...Wars can be prevented as surely as they are provoked. We who fail to prevent them must share the guilt of the dead."

In 1954, a tragedy of his own possessed him. Elizabeth's husband, Hal Beukema, was killed in an airplane crash. Elizabeth was left with two boys, "Hank" and Omar Bradley Beukema, and a daughter Ann. Some time later she remarried and she and her husband had two additional children.

In December, 1965, Mrs. Bradley passed away. General Bradley bore his grief, but he was very lonely. In time he married a young woman, a long-time friend of the family whom he knew well. She was the lovely Kitty Buhler of Los Angeles, California, lecturer and writer.

The United States recognized Omar Bradley's generalship and skill in peace and in war by awarding him the Combat Infantryman's Badge, the Distinguished Service Medal—four times—and fourteen other medals. He also received medals from twelve foreign countries.

In February, 1968, he received the United Service Organization's distinguished service award.

So that thousands could be on hand, the U.S.O. chose to make the presentation in the new Madison Square Garden. When Bradley strode into the packed arena, applause shook the new building. Television cameras highlighted his Lincoln-like features. He stood almost as erect as when, 57 years before, he had reported to Coach Sammy Strang on the diamond at West Point.

When General Emmett O'Donnell of the Air Force stepped into the spotlight with General Bradley, O'Donnell said, "When I was a cadet at West Point, Major Omar Bradley served as an inspiration to all the cadets then and for the rest of his illustrious career. He combined brilliance of military leadership with a tender understanding of the needs of his men, to a degree attained by few others. . . . He truly belongs to the Nation."

Millions thrilled as O'Donnell pinned the U.S.O. medal on Omar Nelson Bradley. He was one of the best-loved and most unique generals ever to win the approval of his countrymen. In peace and war, he had lived up to his title of "The Soldiers' General."

Index